WATERSKIING

A **Waterski International** Guide

Jack Travers
with Chris Boiling

Fernhurst Books

Copyright © Fernhurst Books 1990

First published 1990 by
Fernhurst Books, 31 Church Road, Hove, East Sussex

British Library Cataloguing in Publication Data

Travers, Jack
Waterskiing: a Waterski International guide.
1. Water skiing
I. Title
797.3'5

ISBN 0-906754-51-8

Fernhurst Books would like to thank the British Water
Ski Federation for their help in the preparation of this
book; John Wood for contributing chapters 10 and 11;
Mike Seipel for his barefooting tips; and waterskiers
Danny Budd, Andrew Rooke, Marc Grinhaff, Shawn
Bronson, Mark Turley, Pebbles, Mike Seipel, Louise
Collins, Brett Hodgkins and Daniel Hazelwood, for
allowing themselves to be photographed.

The skier on the front cover is Mick Neville,
photograph by Tom King. The photographs in the text
are by Gavin Newman, Joe McCarthy, Tom King and
Chris Boiling. Fernhurst Books would like to thank
Cypress Gardens for the photographs on pages 2-3, 15
and 91.

Edited and designed by Joyce Chester
Typeset by Central Southern Typesetters, Hove
Printed by Ebenezer Baylis & Son, Worcester
Printed and bound in Great Britain

Contents

Introduction

AT ALL levels, waterskiing is a challenge and a thrill. Whether you are competing in a tournament or just having fun free skiing on a sunny Sunday afternoon, there will always be something new to learn and a new goal to strive for. It might be one more buoy in slalom, one more foot in jumping, a new trick, or perhaps you just want to make your turns tighter and your spray bigger. Whatever it is, this sport will constantly provide you with challenges. You can compete against yourself or against others – the sport is thriving at all levels. At the top end, more and bigger cash prizes are being offered to the professionals. At the other end, millions of recreational skiers are enjoying the thrill of gliding across lakes, rivers and seas, many for the first time.

But, be warned, from the moment you get up, you will be hooked. The sensation of slicing through virgin water is addictive.

It is also a fun way to keep fit and relax. With the sun beating down on your back and the crystal-clear water rushing by below you, your thoughts will be only on skiing.

This book will help you progress quickly to the next stage. At first you will be content with getting up and being towed on two skis.

Then you will see other people carving tight turns on one ski, kicking up great walls of water. You will want to do that. Many skiers are content to stay at that level, others will want to go on to master the slalom course and to learn to trick and jump. This book will help you by explaining the basics in detail. Then it is up to you to go out and practise.

LEFT *Waterskiing can be enjoyed by people of all ages. Here four-year-old Daniel Hazelwood, son of former world champion Mike, practises on a pair of trainer skis.*

Carving tight turns and kicking up great walls of water – for many that is the thrill of waterskiing, for others that is just the beginning.

Tournament skiing

Tournament skiing consists of three events – slalom, figures (tricks) and jump.

Slalom is the classic discipline because it comes closest to what people do while free skiing. In free skiing, skiers zig-zag across the boat's wakes. In slalom, they zig-zag their way through a course of six buoys – three out to the right and three to the left. The boat is driven straight down the centre at a constant speed.

As the skier progresses, the speed goes up to make it more difficult. Once a skier can negotiate all six buoys at the maximum speed – 36 mph (58 km/h) for men and 34 mph (55 km/h) for women – the rope is shortened until the skier falls or misses a buoy. At the world record length of 10.25 m, the rope is 1.25 m shorter than the distance from the centre of the boat to the buoy. At this level the skier has to use his arm as an extension of the rope and lean right over to get round the buoys.

In competitions, slalom is a nail-biting event for spectators because one miss or fall and the skier is out of the event. To succeed requires a combination of technical skill, strength and agility. The top skiers have to accelerate up to 50 mph (80 km/h) to reach the buoys and then slow down quickly to about 15 mph (24 km/h)

to round the buoys, all within a distance of 23 yards (21 m).

Jump is probably the most exciting event for spectators because of the element of danger. When you are travelling at speeds of up to 70 mph (113 km/h) the slightest error can lead to a spectacular crash.

Like slalom, jumping takes place on a pre-set course. The focus of attention is an angled ramp, which is raised and lowered for different age groups. As with slalom, the boat's speed is set at minima and maxima and the aim is to land the furthest distance from the ramp. This is achieved by a combination of speed and lift. The top skiers leave it to the last possible moment before cutting to the ramp, giving them the greatest speed. Once they are on the ramp they have a split second in which to spring off and get maximum height through the air. They have to land safely and ski away to score the distance.

Trick skiing requires a completely different set of skills and is ideal for the smaller, less-strong skier. It may lack the speed, power and inherent danger of the other two events, but it can still enthral the crowds. You can only marvel at the high gymnastic ability of the top skiers as they cram in as many twists, turns

Andrew Rooke executes a perfect flip. Trick skiing may not have the power and speed of slalom or jump, but the skiers can still thrill the crowds with their gymnastic ability.

and flips as possible into two 20-second passes. The harder the trick, the more points it scores. The skier selects his own speed and rope length for this event.

A complicated formula is used to equate the number of buoys rounded on the slalom course with the distance jumped and the number of trick points scored. This way the judges can work out who is the best overall skier at a competition. But the tendency these days is for skiers to specialise in one or two events.

There is certainly enough variety in the three events to keep everyone happy. Once you have become competent at mono skiing, try the slalom course, learn to trick and have a go at jumping. You will not know what you like best until you try them all.

Trick skiing is probably the easiest to learn because you do not need a slalom course or a ramp. The skis are less expensive and you do not need such a powerful boat.

Slalom comes closest to recreational skiing and most skiers like the challenge offered by those six little red buoys floating in the water.

Jumping is probably the easiest event to master at the beginner level and it is not as dangerous as it appears. First time out you will probably be travelling at only 20 mph

(32 km/h) and if you fall off the 5-foot high ramp, it is no worse than falling from a diving board. Water is very forgiving!

Don't be afraid of trying out your new-found skills at a tournament. You may not win but it is a good way of improving. You will learn a great deal just by being around other skiers and, usually, they are a very friendly and helpful group of people. At tournaments it is not uncommon to see 'rivals' offering advice and having a laugh together.

After all, they all started the same way . . .

1. Getting up first time

LEARNING to waterski can be fun. It is one of the easiest and safest sports to learn. Knowing what is about to happen before you try it will help remove most of your fear and apprehension. What is there to be afraid of anyway? Assuming you do not mind getting wet, why not have a go this summer? There is no reason why anyone wanting to learn to ski cannot be skimming across the water in 30 minutes or less.

Guide to choosing your skis

Skier's weight	Boat speed below 30 mph (48 km/h)	Boat speed 30–36 mph (48–58 km/h)	Boat speed above 36 mph (58 km/h)
80–100 lbs (36–45 kg)	64 inches (160 cm)	64 inches (160 cm)	—
100–120 lbs (45–54 kg)	66 inches (165 cm)	64 inches (160 cm)	64 inches (160 cm)
120–140 lbs (54–64 kg)	66 inches (165 cm)	66 inches (165 cm)	64 inches (160 cm)
140–160 lbs (64–73 kg)	68 inches (170 cm)	66 inches (165 cm)	66 inches (165 cm)
160–180 lbs (73–82 kg)	68 inches (170 cm)	68 inches (170 cm)	66 inches (165 cm)
180–200 lbs (82–91 kg)	70 inches (175 cm)	68 inches (170 cm)	68 inches (170 cm)
200–220 lbs (91–100 kg)	70 inches (175 cm)	70 inches (175 cm)	68 inches (170 cm)
220–240 lbs (100–109 kg)	—	70 inches (175 cm)	70 inches (175 cm)

To put skis on, wet your feet and bindings first then slip your toes in as far as possible. Pull up the heel piece as you slide your heel down. The skis being used here are adult combination (combo) skis. The rear binding on the left ski will be used later when you learn to mono ski.

The best way to learn is to visit a waterski club on a warm day with little or no wind blowing.

Your instructor will fit you up with a snug but comfortable nylon-covered buoyancy aid with three buckles which snap together in the front. Next you will be sized up with a pair of fibreglass combo skis with adjustable bindings which the instructor fits properly to your feet. Your bindings will be adjusted tight enough to hold your feet in place but not so tight that they will not release in the event of a fall.

There are three types of skis for novices:

● Trainer skis, used by youngsters up to around four years old.
● Junior combination skis, used by skiers weighing less than 125 lbs (57 kg). These vary in length from 40 to 60 inches (1 to 1.5 m).
● Adult combo skis for skiers weighing over 125 lbs (57 kg). These are 60–80 inches long (1.5–1.75 m).

It's usually better for beginners to learn on skis a bit on the larger size. This will help you to stand up easier at the slower speeds. After you have mastered the start you should resort to smaller skis for more control and manœuvrability.

Having been sized properly, it is time to learn how to ski on dry land.

Stepping into skis is most easily done by wetting both the bindings and your feet. Slip your toes in as far as possible, then reach down and pull up the heel piece as you slide your heel down. Now you are ready to learn the correct basic skiing position.

Learning on land

There are only four things to think about while developing a good skiing position. The easiest way to talk yourself into this posture is to start with your skis and work your way up.

- There should be a space of 6–8 inches (15–20 cm) between your skis. Too much and your skis will tend to split. Too little and you won't have good balance.
- Your knees should be bent forward. They are your shock absorbers and should flex up and down over the waves.
- Push your hips forward. This keeps your weight centred over the middle of the skis.
- Keep your arms straight and at waist level. This is most important and is the thing most beginners forget to do.

The correct skiing position
The key to successful skiing is good body position: knees bent forward, hips pushed forward so the weight is centred over the middle of the skis and arms straight.

The correct skiing position

Note the skis are a comfortable (shoulder) width apart, the arms are straight and holding the handle at waist level and the head is up (not looking down at the water).

The correct grip

This is how you should grip the handle at this stage – with knuckles on top.

Practising on dry land

Former world champion Mike Hazelwood simulates the pull of the boat for a novice at the British Water Ski Federation's training site at Holme Pierrepont, Nottingham.

Now you have a good skiing position, it is time to learn how to arrive there. Sit down on the skis directly behind your heels and lean your chest forward until it touches your knees. Stretch your arms forward around the outside of your knees. At this time your instructor or an aide will pass you a ski handle which you will grasp with both palms facing down. The person with the ski rope represents the tow boat and he will simulate the pull you will receive when you are in the water. As the pull begins you should lean forward slightly onto your toes and begin, slowly and continuously, to straighten your legs until they are slightly bent as they were when you practised the proper skiing position. Once you are standing, check that your elbows are still straight.

Remember to keep your arms extended throughout the entire simulation. Do all of the standing with your legs. Do not pull yourself up with your arms: they are there only to hold onto the handle as you slide through and onto the top of the water.

This exercise should be rehearsed as many times as it takes for you to be certain you understand the procedure.

You can learn to get up on dry land with or without skis. The aim is to arrive at the correct basic skiing position. Let the instructor pull you up. As the pull begins, lean forward slightly and begin to stand up with your legs. Keep your arms straight.

Your first few deepwater starts should be attempted in a minimum water depth of 3–5 feet (1–1.5 m) depending upon your size. It is always easiest if a second person helps you into the proper start position.

In knee-deep water, step into the bindings and shuffle out slowly until the water reaches just above your waist. Lean back a bit so you are floating, helped by your buoyancy aid. Then gently bend your knees, bringing the tips of the skis out of the water. Now you should be in the same position you were in while practising on dry land.

This is the position you should get into in the water, with your knees bent up to your chest, your arms straight and the tips of your skis out of the water. Your lifejacket will keep you afloat.

The deepwater start
Start with towrope between your skis and arms extended around the outside of your knees.

Shout 'Hit it' and wait for the pull of the boat. As the driver accelerates, follow the steps you practised on the shore.

Stand with your legs only. Keep your arms straight by locking your elbows. Maintain a slight bend in your knees.

Keep your head up and push your hips forward so they are directly over your feet and the centre of the skis.

Using a boom

If a boom is available, you will be able to learn the deepwater start quicker. The boom, which extends horizontally from the centre of the boat, is a great confidence-builder. It gives the novice skier something solid to hold while they get the feel for the boat pulling them out of the water.

With the skis extending out of the water approximately 6 inches (15 cm) and 6 inches (15 cm) apart, you should paddle about in the water trying to keep your knees tucked in close to your chest and leaning slightly forward. When you are comfortable and in control in the start position, you are ready to learn to stand up and ski.

With the towrope placed between your skis, your arms extended and around the outside of your knees, your hands gripping the handle with both palms facing down, you're about to experience the thrill of waterskiing. When you are ready, let the boat driver know by shouting, 'Hit it'.

Because slack line is a big problem in the beginning stages, I recommend using a 60-foot (18 m) towrope. As the driver begins to accelerate smoothly and steadily to 18–22 mph (29–35 km/h) you simply follow the steps you practised on the shore. Stand with your legs only. Keep your arms straight by locking your elbows tight. Maintain a slight bend in your knees. And finally, try to centre your hips slightly forward so they are directly over your feet.

Wrong!

Bending the elbows is a common problem and will cause the skier to fall backwards. The answer is to lock those elbows straight.

Common mistakes

Beginners usually make one of two mistakes. Hopefully you will take this as a challenge and be the exception to the rule. They are:

● Bending the elbows and pulling the handle. This seems to be a common reflex action to the boat moving away and causes the skier to fall back.
● As the boat begins to pull ahead, the skier is too anxious and stands up too quickly before there is enough speed for the water to support him. This reaction causes the skier to fall forward.

With any luck, a 'ski boom' may be available. A boom is a bar attached firmly to the side of the boat extending approximately 10 feet (3 m). You should use the same method for coming out of the water but the boom makes the process much easier because it gives you something solid to hold. It is a good confidence-builder.

Once you are up, get the feel for riding across the surface of the water and try to maintain the correct body position: skis 6–8 inches (15–20 cm) apart, knees bent forward, hips pushed forward, arms straight and at waist level.

Wrong!

The knees are bent and the elbows are straight, but this is not the correct skiing position. Push the hips foward so they are over the feet.

2. Skiing on two skis

ONCE you have mastered the deepwater start and can ski comfortably on two skis, you are ready to learn to steer across the wakes.

To begin with, ski from side to side inside the wake. To turn to the left, lean slightly to the left and push on your right ski. Now stop pushing, stand straight, lean a bit to the right and push on your left leg to travel to the right. Practise this until you can travel from the crest of one wake to the crest of the other wake several times in succession.

Steering from side to side is achieved by leaning the way you want to go. Keep your knees bent when crossing the wakes.

Everyone feels more comfortable going in one direction than the other. For the sake of confidence, cross the wake the first time in whichever direction feels easier.

Beginning at the crest of the opposite wake, lean slightly in the direction you wish to travel and push with your outside leg. Continue pushing with your leg until you've gone over the wake and are at least 10 feet (3 m) past it. Stand up and glide for a few feet. When you begin to feel the skis slowing down, lean back towards the wake and push on your other leg

until you've cut back inside the wake. Repeat this drill until you feel confident enough to attempt it on the other wake. Then go across both wakes without stopping in the middle.

There are three major areas of concentration while learning to cross the wakes. They are:

● Keep the handle down low with your arms straight.
● Keep your back straight.
● Take up the shock of the wake with your bent knees.

Don't be afraid of the wakes. They are easy to cross if you remember to keep the handle down low with your arms straight; keep your back straight; and absorb the shock of the wake with bent knees.

3. Mono skiing

ONCE you have learned how to cross both wakes maintaining a good body position, you're ready to take on the challenge of slalom skiing.

Once most beginners have learned to stand up on a pair of skis, they can't wait to slalom. It's great to cut across the wakes and throw up a wall of water as you make sharp turns.

Before attempting slalom skiing, you must decide which foot feels most comfortable to ski on. While skiing behind the boat on two skis, simply shift all of your weight onto one foot, pull up the knee of the other leg and, most importantly, keep the tip of the ski pointing up. Next, perform this same manœuvre with the other leg. After trying this three or four times you will find that you are more stable on one leg than the other. You will drop the ski from the 'less stable' leg.

Using a properly fitted pair of combo skis,

To determine which leg should be your front one on the mono ski, shift all your weight onto one ski and lift the other one clear of the water with the tip pointing up. Next, perform the same manœuvre with the opposite leg. The leg that feels the most stable in the water will become your front one.

Dropping a ski

Shift your weight onto your 'front' leg. Slowly push the drop ski back and, as the binding releases, point your toes down in the water for balance.

When you are stable, place your free foot on the rear toe piece. If you have trouble locating it, slide your free foot down the back of your skiing leg.

Don't rush to put your free foot in the rear toe piece.
Do everything slowly and remember to keep your ski
knee bent.

The correct skiing position

Once you have dropped a ski, this is the position you should aim to be in. Note the position of the feet, legs, knees, arms, hands, handle, back and head.

preferably with one ski rigged with a rear toe binding and deep fin, you are ready to drop a ski. Before setting off, loosen the heel piece of the drop ski so that your foot will lift out more easily.

While skiing in good form (back straight, knees slightly bent, arms straight etc), shift all of your weight onto the ski on which you feel most safe. Slowly push the drop ski back and, as your foot comes out of the binding, point your toes down and place them gently in the water just behind and about 6 inches (15 cm) to the side of your ski foot. You can use your free foot to help stabilise you after your drop ski is gone. Leave your free foot in the water until you feel secure. Very gradually, move your free foot and place it on top of the rear toe piece. If at this time you lose your balance, simply bend your ski knee and place your free foot back in the water, toes down.

Once you can comfortably ride with your back foot on top of the rear toe piece, the next step is to slide your foot inside the binding. The main points are: do every movement as slowly as possible and keep your ski knee bent. Once you have successfully dropped a ski, get the feeling for skiing on just one ski. Fun, isn't it?

Baseball grip

Now is the time to adopt a new grip – the counter or baseball grip where one hand is palm up and the other is palm down. With this new grip it will be easier to make slalom turns.

Once the drop ski is gone, you can use your free foot to help stabilise you. Make sure your toes are pointed down in the water. Leave them there until you have regained your balance.

At this point you are at the level where you need to hold the handle with the counter or baseball grip. If you are skiing with your right foot forward, I recommend you hold the handle with your left hand on top. Left foot forward skiers should begin holding the handle with their right hand on top.

This helps skiers on their weak sides. Skiers standing with their right foot forward have a weak side turn and pull from right to left. Bearing this in mind, you have a stronger pull if your right hand is pulling with the palm facing upward. The same holds true for left foot forward skiers. The weak side pull is stronger if the left hand is pulling with the palm facing upward.

Turning and cutting is done by bending the

Turning and cutting

Turning and cutting is done by bending the knees and leaning in the direction you wish to travel.

Keep your hips forward, handle slightly in and low, and take up the shock of the wake with your bended knees.

knees, while the hips remain forward, and leaning slightly in the direction you wish to travel. Just as with two skis, the beginner should turn and travel from the crest of one side of the wake to the crest of the other side. Once you feel confident enough, you should cross the wake, beginning from the crest of the opposite side, travelling all the way across the wake, keeping the hips forward, handle

slightly in and low and take up the shock of the wake with your knees only.

Always continue travelling past the wake for 10–15 feet (3–4.5 m). Slowly lean back towards the boat, bend your knees a bit, begin to lean more towards the wake and cross it from this direction. Continue to zig-zag across the wakes, making your turns tighter as your ability increases.

4. One ski starts

NOW that you have got the taste for mono skiing, it is time to learn how to start on one ski. There are four basic one ski starts:

- **Deepwater start** with one foot in binding.
- **Deepwater start** with both feet in bindings.
- **Beach start.**
- **Dock start.**

Deepwater start with one foot in binding

The deepwater one foot start differs from two ski starts. Place the towrope on the side of the ski where, previously, you had your second ski. That is the left side if you're about to start on your right foot and the right side if you're about to start on your left foot.

When the rope tightens your arms should be slightly bent. As the boat begins to accelerate to approximately 22 mph (35 km/h) remain crouched with your knee against your chest and lean forward slightly. Because you have only one ski to stand on you should wait at least twice as long to stand up as you did with two skis. Keep your free foot back behind the ski and use it to help guide you as though it were a rudder. As you stand up slowly but continuously, drive your back foot deeper into the water and push your shoulders back away from the boat.

Once you have reached a standing position, maintain a slight bend in your ski leg and slowly put your free foot into the back binding. To avoid the common mistake of standing up too quickly, force yourself to remain in a crouched position for a longer time than you feel is necessary.

Deepwater start with both feet in bindings

Although there is more force pushing against you with two feet in the binding, several beginners – especially lighter skiers – find this technique easiest.

Placing the towrope on the same side as described during the one foot start, bend your knees as much as possible with both feet in the binding. Keep the ski straight in front and at a 45-degree angle to the water as the boat begins to advance. Your only means of controlling the ski is your knees. The more you bend them the more control you have. As you start to move forward through the water, push down with your feet and at the same time push your hips forward over the centre of your front binding.

Deepwater start with one foot in binding

Place the towrope where, previously, you had your second ski. Your front knee should be against your chest and your arms should be slightly bent. As the boat begins to accelerate, lean slightly forward, wait, and stand up when the ski is planing. Keep your free foot behind the ski and dig it deeper in the water as you stand up. At the same time push your shoulders back away from the boat.

Deepwater start with two feet in bindings

Place the towrope on the same side as for a one foot start. Bend your knees as much as possible. Try to keep the ski straight in front of you and at an angle of about 45 degrees to the water as the boat accelerates. As you move forward, push down with your feet, control the ski with your knees and push your hips forward.

Beach start

Stand knee-deep in the water with the ski tip out of the water. Hold a couple of coils of rope. When the rope is tight to the coils drop them and grasp the handle. Yell 'Hit it' and get ready for the boat's pull.

Beach start

In water about knee deep, stand on one leg with your other foot in the binding and raise your ski by bending your knee. With the tip of the ski 4–5 inches (10–13 cm) out of the water and the tail of the ski 4–5 inches (10–13 cm) under the water, you are ready to attempt a beach or shallow water start.

Communication between you and the boat driver is crucial during this type of start. However, it is your responsibility as the skier to give the start signals.

The simplest method is to hold two coils of rope approximately 12 inches in diameter. When the rope is tight to those coils, drop it into the water, grasp the handle, and yell, 'Hit it'. Be prepared for the pull by keeping your arms and ski knee bent. When the boat begins to pull, push forward slightly in the direction of the boat.

There are two important factors to bear in mind when you are using this particular start. Firstly, you must communicate verbally with the driver. Secondly, don't 'jump the gun'. (Many novices react to the roar of the engine.) This start differs from the two deepwater starts in that there is a definite delay between the boat starting and you, the skier, starting. The boat begins first and not until the rope tightens do you push forward and ski away.

Dock start

This is very similar to the beach start. Once again it is crucial that you communicate verbally with the driver. Sit on the edge of the dock with the tip of the ski pointing up slightly, arms and ski knee bent. Hold two coils of rope, 12 inches in diameter, just as in the shallow water start. When the rope tightens, drop the coils into the water, yell 'Hit it' and prepare to be pulled off the dock. As you touch the water, keep your knees bent, handle low (waist high), and lean back away from the pull of the boat.

Equipment

The same equipment used for mono skiing should be used in learning one ski starts.

If the ski seems to have too much drag, then simply try a wider or flatter bottomed ski. The wider the ski, the easier it is to come out of the water. Once you have mastered a start on the bigger ski, you can gradually work down to the smaller appropriate size.

Having conquered at least one of the slalom starts, you should be truly proud of yourself. Learning to get up on one ski is an achievement that looks much easier than it actually is.

Now is the time to choose a real slalom ski

Dock start

Sit on the dock with the ski tip pointing up. Hold a couple of coils of rope, like a beach start. Let the boat pull you off the dock – as it does so bend your knees, keep handle low and lean away from boat.

and find out what skiing is all about. Note that I say choose not buy! There are many brands and models available and I recommend that you test ride as many as possible before deciding which one suits you best.

5. Slalom skiing

THE easiest and least discouraging method of learning to ski the slalom course is to go through the half or mini course first. It gives you the challenge of skiing around buoys and crossing the wakes several times in succession without feeling as though it is totally impossible to get from one buoy to the next.

What is the half course?

The boat travels at approximately 22–24 mph (35–39 km/h) midway between the right-hand boat gates and the turn buoys on the right side of the course. As the boat begins to pass the first gate, you should begin to lean to the right and ski outside the wake approximately 20 feet (6 m). As you approach the first buoy on the right side, you will be about 5 feet (1.5 m) wide of the buoy and should begin your turn to the left at least 10 feet (3 m) before you arrive at the buoy. The buoy is the point where you *finish*, not begin, the turn.

As you pass the buoy you should have

Before you can ski the full course, you need to get used to cutting and turning at pre-set intervals. That's where the half course comes in.

The layout and dimensions of a regulation slalom course.

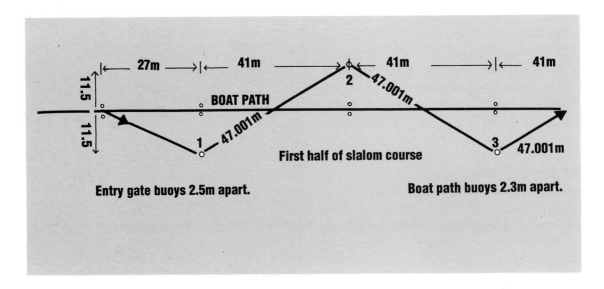

finished your turn and be concentrating on your pulling position. Keep leaning to the left with the handle down low, hips slightly forward and knees flexed. Continue this lean through both wakes. Once you pass the second wake, let up on your pull. The ski will glide a bit then begin to slow. You should be approaching the boat gate on the left side of the wake. As you feel the ski slowing, bend your knees a bit and begin to lean to the right as you pass between the two boat gate buoys.

Now repeat the pulling position, this time to the right side.

Problems

If you find that you are not getting to the buoy early enough to begin your turn before it, then try being a bit more aggressive with your lean through the wakes. This will give you a bit more angle and get you across the wakes quicker with a bit more speed.

Slack line is a common problem. It is generally caused by either skiing too upright with straight legs or pulling too long.

Since the mini course is designed to teach skiers how to cross the wakes several times in rapid succession, the most common cause of slack line at this point is pulling too long.

The next step

When you can negotiate the mini course consistently, you should attempt to ski around the boat gate rather than through it.

Continue learning on the mini course until you can manage it easily at a speed of about 24 mph (39 km/h) on a 60-foot (18 m) towrope.

Then tackle the full slalom course at a boat speed of between 20–24 mph (32–39 km/h). First cross the wakes from left to right at least 10 feet (3 m) before the entrance gates. As you cross the second wake, make certain that you remain on your pulling or right edge of the ski for at least 10 feet (3 m). Stop your pull, begin to lean back toward the wake and bend your knees. You will feel the ski glide at this point. When the glide is over and the ski is decelerating, begin your turn to the left.

If you go around the buoy with a tight line, you have timed your pull properly. Slack line

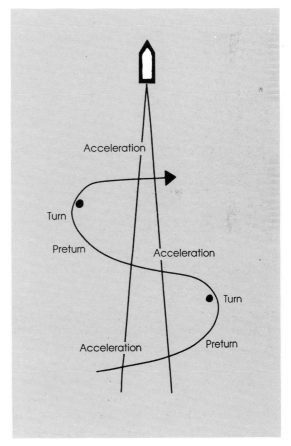

The three phases of slalom skiing: acceleration, deceleration and turning.

*When you can negotiate the half course consistently,
you should attempt to ski around the boat gate
rather than through it.*

at this stage means you need to stop pulling sooner so that you begin to decelerate sooner. Should you make your turn inside the buoy, then you must hold your edge a bit longer after the second wake. Remember, the buoy is the point where the turn is finished, not started.

Smooth slalom skiing can only be accomplished by pulling extremely hard through the wakes. If you pull too hard just after the turn you will probably not be able to hold your direction through the wakes and the boat will make you stand up. However, beginning the pull or lean easier allows you to increase your speed and hold your direction as you cross the wakes. In short, gradually increase your pull so it is at its maximum as you cross between the wakes.

Often, when a skier has managed the number one buoy turn, he cannot seem to come round the number two buoy early enough to reach the third buoy. In this case, simply begin the course in the same manner with number two buoy. Cross the wakes from right to left just before the number one buoy gate and use the same technique as performed for number one buoy.

When you are able to negotiate all six buoys

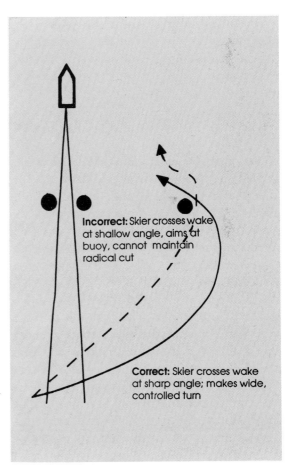

Turning at a buoy.

every time you cross the wakes before the entrance gates, you should make your turn a little later until finally you are going through the entrance gates just left of the right-hand gate buoy.

The entrance gate

The slalom course begins long before the entrance gate. Your initial pull to the left sets the tone for how wide and early you will be for your turns inside the course. The set up pull should be early enough so that you will be wide enough yet decelerating into your turn for the gate.

How wide is wide enough? The answer is: you can never get too wide in slalom.

Often skiers say, 'But I was so wide I couldn't turn my ski.' Have you felt that? In most cases it's not the width that's causing that feeling but the speed. This is why your goal is to be wide, but early enough so that you are slowing into your turn. The chances are pretty good that if you are moving fast into your turn for the gate you will carry similar speed into your turn for number one buoy.

Ideally you should be wider than buoys 2, 4 and 6 on the left side of the course.

The reason for being wider is so that when you finish the turn you will be lined up with the left-hand row of buoys.

The approach

The pull for the gate must be progressive. If you are moving fast as you approach the gate you will have to turn fast and begin to pull hard to make it through the gate. It is impossible to make a progressive pull to the gate if you have already pulled your hardest just after the turn.

You will always have a better chance of having a decent gate by being too early rather than too late.

Most people would say that missing the entrance gate in practice is a bad thing which develops into a bad habit. I also believed this for many years. Now I think it does not matter.

If, after you have made your turn for the gate and are into your pull, you feel that you are too early, go ahead and miss the gate rather than flatten off to make it through the gate. By flattening off, you are practising improper slalom technique. Remember, this is practice and practice is for learning. By missing the gate you have learned something. On your next approach you can adjust by turning a bit later or slower.

The entrance gate

Pull to the left early enough so you can decelerate into the turn for the gate. Your pull for the gate should be progressive. Aim to go through the gate just left of the right-hand buoy.

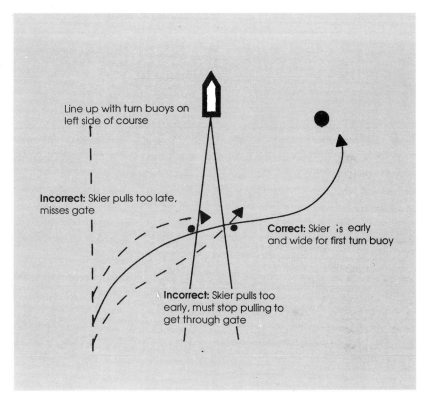

Line up with turn buoys on left side of course

Incorrect: Skier pulls too late, misses gate

Correct: Skier is early and wide for first turn buoy

Incorrect: Skier pulls too early, must stop pulling to get through gate

Advanced techniques

Before the foil (also called the wing) was introduced skiers began their edge change immediately as they came across the second wake. Now, because of the drag caused by the foil mounted on the fin, advanced skiers can ski the course much wider. Due to the extra drag when the skier pulls, even in excess of 10 feet (3 m) past the second wake, the ski begins to decelerate almost immediately.

Always feel your pulling edge dig into the water after the second wake. If that edge doesn't dig in you are on a flat ski – and you should never be on a flat ski when you are slalom skiing. This feeling of digging in just after the second wake marks the end of the pull and the beginning of the edge change.

When you are changing from the pulling edge to the turning edge, there are two things to think about.

● Relax your knees. During your pull, push with your legs. As you finish your pull bend your knees slightly.

Former world junior champion, Brett Hodgkins, makes an aggressive, progressive pull for the entrance gate.

● Keep your outside hand on the handle. What does this do? By keeping your outside hand on the handle you are eliminating the chance of riding on a flat ski. The boat actually helps to bring you onto your inside edge. Always change your edge first and reach second.

Once you have made this edge change you are ready to begin your reach, which is the beginning of the turn. The turn is divided into three phases:

The reach
Keep the line tight as you start the reach: this helps make the turn much smoother. Don't extend your arm completely; try to keep your elbow bent. This brings your ski onto more of the edge which helps keep the rope tight. As you approach the buoy, extend your arm enough to go around it.

Turning
The three main points to remember about your position in the turn are:

● Handle high.
● Knees bent.
● Head up.

Keeping the handle high keeps the ski on its turning edge. Dropping the handle causes a slamdunk turn.

Why does every coach tell you to keep your knees bent in the turn? Everyone knows that is what is supposed to happen, but why? Assuming that you have bent your knees before beginning your turn, if you straighten them before you finish turning most likely one of two things will happen.

● The ski will rear up in front of you causing a delay in the turn.
● You will break forward at the waist.

Whichever is the case, you've lost valuable time in the turn.

Keeping your head up helps you keep your knees bent. Dropping your head or looking down causes you to straighten your legs. This involuntary reaction is not at all limited to slalom skiing.

To finish answering the question of why have your knees bent in the turn I need to move into the final phase of the turn.

Preparing for the pull
You should finish the turn by rotating your outside hip around and bringing the handle

down to meet it. Now comes the hard part: most skiers as they rotate the hip also react with their knees. If you straighten your legs as you finish the turn you limit your pull to your upper body only. Whereas if you are able to concentrate on keeping your knees bent until you have finished the turn, not only do you have your upper body to lean with, but the power of your legs to push with.

Through the wakes

When you have completed the turn you are ready to begin your push to and through the wake. Note push, not pull. This is where you win or lose. Remember, the harder you start the more difficult it is to make your push progressive. Always begin your push with enough force but not so much that you cannot increase your push and lean so that it peaks as you cut across and through the second wake. As you cross the second wake feel your back edge dig into the water and then begin your edge change.

Pushing with your legs as you begin your lean to and through the wakes is quite simply a more powerful method of applying your strength.

This technique may seem difficult at first

Skiing the course

Marc Grinhaff pulls wide and sets himself up for the entrance gate and then demonstrates the various phases of slalom skiing – cutting, gliding, turning (accelerating, decelerating and turning) – as he rounds the first two buoys.

A good way of getting back into the swing of things after a lay-off is two-hand skiing at a slower speed than normal – as Danny Budd demonstrates here.

but there is a simple way of experiencing it and mastering it if you are willing to sacrifice a bit of time. Believe me, it will pay off in the long run.

While out for your normal day of training, once you have reached your trouble pass, be it with a rope length of 18.25 m or 12 m (15 off or 35 off), try concentrating on this push and lean method. If you can't get past number two buoy drop your speed 1 full mph (1.5 km/h). If you still have problems getting to number three buoy drop your speed again. Never be embarrassed about slowing the boat speed at

your trouble pass: after all training is for learning not for practising the same mistakes.

After a lay-off

Every spring so many skiers who, at the end of the previous season, were running 13–14.25 m (28–32 off) have trouble getting around the first buoy. So, for those of you who have had a long lay-off, here are a few ideas about getting back into the slalom course without falling around number one buoy four times in a row, wondering if maybe someone swapped skis with you during the winter, or maybe you forgot to put your fin back on.

What you should do after a long lay-off is simply start the course without the entrance gates and ski around the buoys, trying to get the feeling back at a lower speed, say 32 or 31 mph (52–50 km/h).

Once you have made a couple of passes in a row without the gates, try one pass crossing the wakes from left to right, just before them. Gradually work your way closer until you are passing through them.

It is less frustrating in the long run to swallow your pride and work on style. I realise that your season is short and you must get back into it as quickly as possible, but when

Defining the length of the towrope

In North America the length of the towrope is given as feet off the standard 75-foot rope length. In Europe the actual length of the towrope is given, in metres.

Europe	North America	Colour
18.25 m	15 off	red
16.00 m	22 off	orange
14.25 m	28 off	yellow
13.00 m	32 off	green
12.00 m	35 off	blue
11.25 m	38 off	pink
10.75 m	39½ off	white

the water is cold it is better to ski than swim.

Another exercise to work on during the early part of the year is two-hand skiing at 14.25 m (28 off) at 4 mph (6 km/h) below your maximum speed.

Ever since the introduction of the foil, the biggest mistake skiers make is under-pulling. This method of short-line slalom skiing at slower speeds forces you to pull long to reach the buoy yet, because of the speed, reaching the buoy is not impossible. I used this system on a student of mine. He persevered with it for about three weeks. His rope length was actually 13 m (32 off) and his boat speed 32 mph (51 km/h). On the Friday of the third week, he began his second set at 16 m (22 off) at 36 mph (58 km/h) and ran through to 3 at 12 m (35 off).

Now this score was not something he had not been able to do before, but his style was drastically improved and his 13 m (32 off) pass was negotiated with a tight line. The point I am trying to make is that if you take a bit of time to work on style and technique, even if it means dropping the speed, at least you are skiing and not swimming. The more time you spend on the water, the more you learn.

I don't claim to be the originator of this exercise, I just use it because it works. Not only does it work for the advanced skier, but it also teaches the intermediate skier the proper pull.

6. Wake jumping

JUMPING the wakes on a slalom ski is not something done to score points in a competition, but is spectacular, exhilarating and just plain good fun. It is important to always enjoy your waterskiing!

As you finish a turn, make a gentle cut so that you can maintain control as you approach the wake. With your knees well bent and your upper body centred over your bindings, let off on your pull just before you reach the wake and push with both legs just as the toes of your front foot reach the crest of the wake.

Try for just a little bit of air the first time. As you get the feel for it, you can begin by cutting from a bit further away, building up more speed, pushing harder with your legs and travelling higher and further through the air.

You should always enjoy your skiing – wake jumping is a good way to have fun. Cut to the wake, keep your knees bent, ease off the pull just before the wake and then, as your front foot reaches the crest of the wake, push off with both legs – as Shawn Bronson does here.

7. Learning tricks

TRICK skiing can be one of the most enjoyable and fulfilling forms of waterskiing. As always, however, there are a few important factors in the early sessions which can either lead to success or frustrating failure.

Here are the keys to making trick skiing fun:

● Make certain that your skis are the proper size and the bindings are mounted and fitted properly.
● Know how to perform each trick before you attempt it.
● Understanding and communication between you, the observer and the 'experienced' boat driver.

Skis will range in length from 36 inches (91 cm) for children to 44 inches (112 cm) for large adults. Use the table below as a guide to choosing your skis for tricks. The bindings should fit securely so that your heel remains down when you bend your knees forward. Binding placement should be such that your ankle bone is in the centre of the ski.

With the skis set up properly, it's time to try them out and get the feel of how to control these unusual looking skis with no stabilising fins on the bottom. It helps to have an experienced boat driver who will know to pull you slowly out of the water and maintain a constant slow boat speed – 10–18 mph (17–29 km/h) depending on your size and weight.

The first five to ten minutes on trick skis should be spent acquiring a good solid body position. To achieve this, stand as straight as possible on your skis, bend your knees forward and bend your ankles slightly. Bend your arms slightly to take up any shock from the boat's pull and push the handle down towards your waist.

Guide to choosing your trick skis

Skier's weight	Ski size
40–80 lbs	36 inches
18–36 kg	91 cm
80–110 lbs	38 inches
36–50 kg	97 cm
110–130 lbs	40 inches
50–59 kg	102 cm
130–160 lbs	42 inches
59–73 kg	107 cm
over 160 lbs	44 inches
over 73 kg	112 cm

British team member, Andrew Rooke, demonstrates the basic position on two trick skis.

At first, you should try to ski slowly back and forth inside the wake making sure not to force the skis one way or the other. Once you feel confident and in control, you may attempt to cross whichever wake feels easier. As you cross the top, keep your knees bent forward and the handle down low. When you can cross both wakes and feel you know how the skis will react, you are ready to try your first trick – the side slide.

The side slide

For this trick hold the handle with your knuckles facing up. Before attempting to turn the skis, try pulling the handle slowly in and down without moving your shoulders. If you feel your body slide forward and accelerate a bit, you have executed this movement properly. If you do not feel this sliding effect, chances are you brought your shoulders down as you pulled the handle in. Try it again and keep your shoulders up. This pulling action is the first and most important part of every trick.

Now let's try the side slide along with the pull. Slowly pull the rope in and down. As you begin to feel the skis slide, bend your knees a little more and turn the skis to one side. As the skis begin to turn, let go with your back

The side slide

Pull the rope in and down, bend your knees and turn your skis to one side. As the skis begin to turn, let go with the back hand.

hand. Allow the skis to slide just a bit and return to the front. Well, if you made it the first time – *great!* If not, let's analyse what went wrong before trying again.

The biggest problem with teaching beginners the side slide is that they are afraid of falling so they won't turn their skis enough and travel across rather than slide. Don't be afraid of falling. The best trick skiers in the world fall and learn from their falls. Go ahead and turn your skis sideways and see what happens.

Once in the side slide position, there is really only one of four things that can happen.

● You fall away from the boat because you pulled the handle too high and leaned too far away from the boat.
● The leading edge of your back ski digs in and the ski comes off because your skis were too far apart when you started to turn.
● The leading edge of your front ski digs in because you didn't pull the rope in first or bend enough as you turned.
● You slide sideways completing the trick.

The side slide is the building block of all your tricks. To recap:

180 front to back

Use your knees to turn the skis 90 degrees further than you did for the side slide. Pull the handle into your back and regrasp it with your back hand.

1. Pull handle in and down slowly.
2. Slide, bend more and turn.
3. Let go with back arm.
4. Keep handle low with arm bent, to absorb the 'shock'.
5. Start the trick with your knees slightly bent and finish with them bent more.

Having mastered the side slide, repeat this process and learn the reverse immediately. The reverse will be a bit more difficult. However, if you can analyse the problem by using the check list above, you can work out the solution for yourself.

Here are some more basic tricks which are fun to learn and impressive to perform.

180 front to back

Having mastered both side slides, with proper position and technique, the 180-degree turn from front to back should not be much of a problem. Because you are going to turn 90 degrees further, your pull on the handle needs to be slightly stronger. Once you have released the handle with your back arm, continue turning the skis to the back with your knees. Pull the handle into your back grasping it with your other hand. At this point you should

180 back to front
*Let go with one hand, keep the handle in close to
your body and let the boat pull you round.*

make certain that you are looking up, bending
your knees slightly and your hands are touch-
ing the small of your back.

A common problem is falling away from the
boat. This is generally caused by straightening
your legs during or at the finish of the turn. If
you fall towards the boat, either your pull was
not strong enough or you let the handle out
when you arrived in the back position.

180 back to front

Because you are returning to a familiar position, the 180-degree turn from back to front is
probably the easiest basic trick to learn. It is
the first time you will complete a trick arriving

in a position which you have been in previously.

Simply by letting go with one hand and
keeping the handle in close to your body, the
pull of the boat will return you to the front
position. But, as the boat begins to pull you to
the front, keep your knees bent, your head up
and the handle in close. The most common
mistake is letting the handle out away from
the body as you begin to turn.

Having become accomplished at the 180-
degree turn from front to back and back to
front, follow these same instructions and learn
the reverse of these tricks. Execution of these
tricks slowly and properly is of utmost importance at this stage.

The basic position on one ski. Note the closeness of the feet, the flexed knees, handle at waist height and weight centred over the feet.

360 front to front

The 360-degree front to front turn is performed by merely executing a 180-degree turn from front to back and as you grab the handle with your free hand in the back position, pull the handle toward your back a bit, let go with your initial turning hand and continue to turn around to the front. Areas of concentration in this trick are:

● A good steady pull.
● Head up.
● Keep the handle in close.

As with all previous tricks, follow up by learning the reverse.

One ski tricks

Before learning any one ski tricks, I strongly recommend riding on two skis in the back position. While skiing backwards, try travelling slowly back and forth inside the wake. As I mentioned earlier, returning to a familiar position in tricks is always easier than turning into an unfamiliar position. So why not learn the back to front 180-degree turn on one ski first?

180 turn

Once you have learned to ride on one ski in the forward position, turn around backwards on two skis. After obtaining a good solid position, lean onto the ski you slalom on and try taking your weight off your drop ski. Don't lift the ski until you feel confident that you can stand alone on your slalom foot. The next step is to loosen the heel of your drop ski, turn to the back, slowly lean onto your slalom foot and let your drop ski slide off. Initially, you should drag your free foot in the water for stability. When you are in control, slowly move your free foot over towards your ski and place it on the ski just behind your ski foot. If at any point you begin to lose your balance, simply remove your back foot from the ski and place it gently on the water to regain control.

Once you are comfortable riding backwards with your foot on the ski, you are ready to learn the basic one ski tricks in this order:

- Back to front.
- Side slide.
- Reverse side slide.
- Front to back.
- Reverse back to front.
- Reverse front to back.
- 360 front to front.
- Reverse 360 front to front.

The guidelines mentioned earlier for two ski tricks also apply to one ski tricks. But because your weight is being supported by only half as much ski area, the pull for advancement is twice as important. Also, because of the lack of ski surface, flexibility in the knees is more important for control and balance.

180 turn

Ski backwards on two skis, shift your weight over your 'front' foot and drop the other ski. Slowly move *your free foot over towards your ski and place it on the ski just behind your ski foot.*

180 back to front

See how the positions learned while doing the two *ski side slide and 180 turns help when it comes to doing the same tricks on one ski.*

*Rising British star, Corinna Williams,
demonstrates a tricky toe hold.*

Advanced tricks

The top skiers divide their two 20-second trick passes into hand and toe passes. One way they do as many tricks as possible holding onto the handle with their hands, the other way they keep hold of the towrope with one foot firmly placed in the toe strap.

Before learning toe tricks, make sure you have an experienced driver and 'quick release' person in the boat and a 'quick release' device attached to the ski pylon. In the event of a fall the rope can be released from the boat and you won't be dragged along behind it if you can't get your foot out of the toe strap.

Toe turns

The method of teaching toe turns varies from one instructor to another. Some believe that all tricks should be done with the knee bent in the beginning and remaining that way throughout the trick. Others teach that you should start with your leg bent, come up or unweight as you turn and then drop back down as you finish.

I have a somewhat different theory. I coach people to be comfortable and relaxed at the beginning of each trick and concentrate as they go into it. A comfortable position is not stand-ing on a ski with your ski leg bent and your toe leg trying to hold the strap within 12 inches of your knee.

Rather I teach the student to stand with his ski leg straight and toe leg extended before attempting any trick.

Beginning all tricks from this position means you start with a straight body axis, which is important. Standing with your ski leg straight gives you this upright stance. This straight leg start also stops you turning with your upper body. From this position you will find it virtually impossible to turn the ski without bending your knee.

Advancement is the start of every trick except where you may be unwrapping from the rope. But if your toe leg is in close from the start it will make it most difficult, if not impossible, to pull yourself forward or towards the boat.

Let's pause for just a moment here and discuss and define advancement. Advancement in trick skiing is the strong, slow pull the skier must make prior to making his turn and com-leting the trick.

The amount of pull will depend on how many degrees the turn will be. Obviously the more rotation, the harder the pull should be.

Toe side slide (and reverse)

Place your foot in the toe strap and assume a relaxed stance. Bend your ski leg slightly and then pull your toe leg in towards your thigh slowly but firmly. Lead the turn with your knee followed by your hips.

Why must there be advancement?

This may sound like a simple question but, when asked, many skiers will say it's just part of the trick. Think of it this way: while you are executing the trick the boat is travelling forward. If you do not pull yourself forward prior to your turn, you will either lose your straight position or the handle itself because the handle and rope are being pulled by the boat.

What we have been describing so far are basics, fundamentals which, if learned in the early stage of trick skiing, allow for the more difficult tricks to be absorbed more easily at a later date.

Often a student arrives at my ski school with the ability of executing high point trick runs, possibly as much as 5000 points, but because several of the tricks may have been learned without paying particular attention to basic body position, improvement from this point may be very difficult.

You are never a great enough trick skier that you don't need to check on yourself from

time to time and make sure your basic body position is correct. More often than not you will find this is where a problem lies. It is the foundation on which everything is built.

Before attempting these more difficult manœuvres I cannot overemphasise the importance of having an extremely competent release person and qualified driver. It's just too easy to get hurt unnecessarily.

Before learning the toe side slide you should spend a bit of time holding a reverse side slide and removing your back foot from the ski.

Believe me, this sounds a lot easier than it actually is. With your back foot resting on top of, or between, your front and rear toe piece, turn to the reverse side slide position and remove your rear foot from the ski.

There is no need to try turning into the reverse side slide position while standing with only one foot on the side as this is more difficult than the actual reverse toe side slide.

Once you feel confident sliding on one foot you are ready for the toe hold.

Place your foot into the toe strap and assume

The toe side slide is the building block to more advanced tricks like this.

the relaxed stance I spoke of earlier. Ready to begin? Bend your ski leg slightly and then pull your toe leg in towards your thigh slowly but firmly. Let your leg back out and relax again.

This is what I call the pre-pull or the pre-paration pull. It gives your body a chance to get used to the sensation of this manœuvre.

Repeat this pull again and again making certain as you pull that your shoulders remain back away from the boat and that your hips and knee come forward first.

When you feel confident that you are bringing your hips and knee forward, and not your shoulders down, as you make your advancement then you are ready for the turn.

All this should be led with your knee or knees followed by your hips, then shoulders and head. Leading with the head and shoulders, as formerly taught, causes the upper body to bend and bring you off your straight axis.

Make one preparation pull to check your position. Assuming you maintained a good straight position you are ready for the turn. Bend your ski knee slightly in order to maintain control during the pull. Draw the toe leg in firmly and, once you feel the ski begin to slide, turn the ski by dropping deeper in your knee and turning your hips. For side slides there is absolutely no need to rotate your shoulders or head.

Once you become skilled at this trick, you will have a solid foundation to go on and learn other toe turns.

8. Learning to jump

DOESN'T everyone love long distance jumping? Surely it is the one event that every spectator can feel in the pit of his stomach.

Do you ever wonder if the best jumpers are just especially gifted, whether there's one single ingredient that makes them what they are? As an instructor to numerous beginners and the best jumpers in the world today, I can never over-emphasise the importance of the proper procedures in training and progress. Every top jumper has had to advance through all of the various stages before obtaining success.

Beginning jumping

Novices should start by going over the bottom right-hand corner of the ramp first. This way you get to feel the surface of the ramp without the fear of dropping from 5 feet (1.5 m) in the air and there is far less chance of your falling on the ramp surface.

The boat driver should take a path as close as possible to a 45-degree angle to the ramp. A simple method of determining whether the direction is correct is as follows: as the boat driver approaches the ramp from left to right at approximately 30 feet (9 m) from the bottom

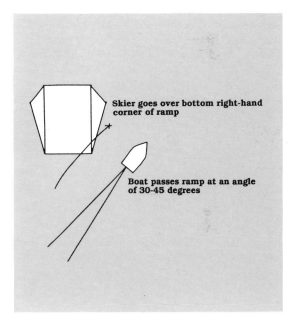

The corner jump technique.

he should not be able to see the side curtain until he is nearly at the ramp. As he goes by the ramp he should go directly between the inside and the outside guide buoys. I've always found it helpful for a boat driver to try to familiarise himself with the surroundings by making a few passes at the ramp from this angle before taking the new jumper.

Essential equipment for jumpers

All jumpers should wear a proper suit with built-in padding and flotation and a purpose-made crash helmet. Top skiers also wear an armsling to keep their right arm in. The skis are strong and light – and expensive.

About 80 per cent of those wishing to learn how to jump have been on a slalom ski ever since they learned how to drop a ski, so the chances are they will feel awkward for the first ten to fifteen minutes back on two skis again.

Lesson number one for the new jumper: make sure you are comfortable and in control of your skis. Ride around on them for a while and jump the wakes. When you are confident and you know you can manage the jump, it is time for some dry land instruction.

The simplest way to explain is to start at the bottom – the skis – and build up from there.

Your skis should be shoulder width apart. Too wide and they will spread. Too close and there is a loss of balance. Your knees should be bent forward so that you feel a tightening in your calf muscles and your ankles.

The handle should be held with the left palm up and the right palm down, brought in just below the waist.

Bend slightly forward at the waist, making sure not to push your backside out but enough to bring your shoulders just forward of your knees. Keep your head up.

Go over this position with the skis on until

Correct body position on ramp
Skis shoulder width apart, knees bent, body bent slightly forward at the waist, head up and handle held with left palm up, right palm down.

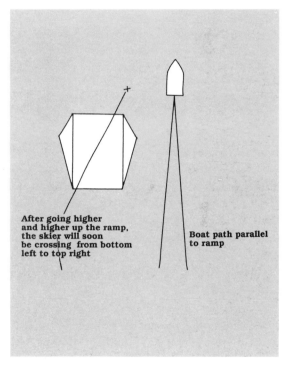

After going higher and higher up the ramp, the skier will soon be crossing from bottom left to top right

Boat path parallel to ramp

Boat and skier paths for the first jump.

you know it – and I mean really know it. It is then a good idea to ride around on the water, directing and maintaining yourself in this position, before your first attempt at the ramp.

Beginning approximately 100 feet (30 m) from the ramp, lean to the left and remain roughly 30 feet (9 m) from the wake. As you come within 25 feet (7.5 m) of the ramp's bottom right-hand corner, make a conscious effort to shift an equal amount of weight onto the left ski and bend a little lower in the knees. Most beginners' falls are caused by bringing the handle above the waist. See if you can beat the odds. When you cross the corner, push the handle down to your thighs – it will help keep your shoulders forward and your weight over your skis.

The first couple of times across the corner use as little of the ramp as possible so as to experience merely what the surface feels like.

Once you can travel across the corner in good form, the instructor should tell you to go a little higher after each successful pass. As

Get a feel for the ramp by skiing over the bottom right-hand corner. Approach at an angle of 30–45 degrees. Keep your shoulders forward and your weight over your skis.

you go higher over the side of the ramp the driver should begin straightening out his boat.

After one or two outings you will be skiing from the bottom left-hand corner of the jump to the top right-hand corner, and the rest is easy.

Making progress

Once you have got to the stage where you can successfully ride up the centre of the ramp and land solidly in good form for 10 jumps in a row it's time to begin the single wake cut, which leads you to the spring, pop or jam.

The boat path at this point should be a straight line parallel to the ramp surface, approximately 5 feet (1.5 m) in from the inside guide buoy. You merely need to make a few minor adjustments to the position which by now should feel natural. Without the use of

the ramp you should learn how to cut or edge in the following manner. Standing just outside the left-hand wake, in the precise stance you have already learned, you should exert downward pressure to the inside of your right knee, thus dropping the left edge of the right ski deeper into the water. At the same time you should lower your left shoulder away from the pull of the boat. This shoulder movement also drops the left edge of the left ski deeper into the water. This action will allow you to travel slowly away from the boat, in a controlled fashion. Practise this a few times until it feels comfortable.

Using this technique, you should start your edge to the ramp early enough so that you can make an easy progression into the centre of the jump. Your aim should be to make contact with the ramp in the centre and leave the jump close to the top left-hand corner. It is vital that you begin early and slowly so that the direction is always from the boat.

It is important that you make no adjustments until you have executed this manœuvre at least ten times in good order, with a tight rope and solid landings.

At this point you should be told that the boat is going to be moved outward from the ramp, to just inside the inside guide buoy, but that you only need to edge a little harder 'into the ramp' and should not begin the cut any earlier than before.

The boat speed should gradually be increased only if you maintain a slow start and gradually progressive cut. After the boat speed has reached 28 mph (45 km/h) for juniors and 30 mph (48 km/h) for all others, the path should be moved outside the inside guide buoy. If at any time you begin to lose your controlled progressive edge to the ramp, I advise the boat driver to lower the speed 2 mph (3 km/h) until you regain that control.

Every step forward in jumping is important but this stage is critical and requires more time and patience. You should not attempt to go any faster or jump any further than the speed and ramp height will physically allow.

Correct body position for edging
Exert downward pressure on the inside of your right knee and lower the left shoulder away from the pull of the boat.

Making a progressive cut to the ramp, aiming for the centre and leaving close to the top left-hand corner. The spring is an extension to the cut and a *natural reaction to the change in surfaces – from water to ramp. Bend your knees on landing.*

I mentioned earlier that while learning the single wake cut you also learn to spring. As you edge harder all the way to the ramp you are pushing with your knees to go away from the boat and reach the centre of the ramp. There is far more pressure and drag in the water than on the ramp surface so that as you are leaning away from the boat and pushing with your legs when you reach the ramp there is a re-action as the pressure is released from the water and the kick or spring is simply an extension of the cut.

One final word for jumpers at this level: do not increase the boat speed nor move the boat out away from the jump if you are not making contact with the ramp within 2 feet (60 cm) of the centre. If you are edging all the way to the ramp then the rope remains tight and the boat is pulling you so that you will not travel 6 feet (1.8 m) across during the split second spent on the jump.

Advanced jumping

Generally speaking the advanced jumper is one who has progressed from the single wake cut to the double wake cut. This is a level where all jumpers should, and the great jumpers have, remained for an extremely long period of time. It is during this stage that you develop a sense of timing. You begin to look at the ramp from a different angle and a greater distance.

To begin the double wake cut you use virtually the same method as the single wake cut. Start your approach early enough so that you

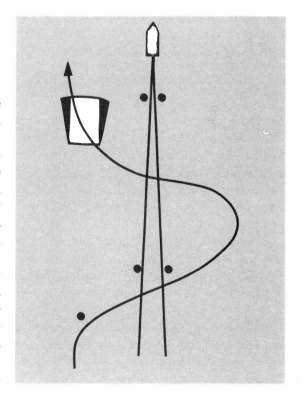

The double wake cut.

can hold a slow but progressive edge from the finish of the turn, through the wakes and all the way into the centre of the ramp.

Begin the first double wake cut from approximately 15–20 feet (4.5–6 m) to the right of the wake. This distance is not too far to frighten you yet far enough to allow good visibility between you and the jump. Beginning the cut from this point you will also develop more of a turn and a better edge through the wake. Starting the cut closer to the wake is usually more favourable to the jumper, but the boat will be blocking the line of sight. The closer you are to the centre of the line of the boat the more difficult it is to turn your skis and set your edge.

When a skier attempts a double wake cut

Advanced jumpers use a double wake cut. This gives them the speed that is necessary to cut wide and overtake the tow boat. Then, if they time their turn correctly, they will almost be catapulted on to the ramp. It is this speed into the ramp and the lift off it which gives them their great distances.

for the first time he may experience a moment of panic. He tends to turn his skis a bit too hard and ends up arriving at the ramp early on flat skis. So, if during your first attempt at the double wake cut the pull does not feel the same into the jump as the single wake pull did, pass.

Once you can manage the double wake cut from this distance start moving out further from the wake about 5 feet (1.5 m) at a time.

When you have accomplished, with a good amount of self assurance, a double wake cut from 35-45 feet (10.5-13.7 m) from the right of the centre line of the boat it is time to begin increasing the speed of the boat. This, how-ever, does not apply to junior girls or boys who will already have reached their maximum boat speed at this point.

Boat speed increases should always be as gradual as possible so you are not startled into making uncontrolled movements during the approach to the ramp. If you lose the solid progressive cut and good strong edge into the centre of the ramp surface, boat speed must be decreased until you regain control.

Although the advanced stage of jumping, the double wake cut, does not seem to have taken long to break down into simple learning stages it is without doubt a period when you must consolidate your timing and control before you can hope to survive advancing to the next stage, that of the superstars.

How jump distances are measured

Judges at meter stations A, B, and C record the angle of the landing in relation to the ramp. These readings are converted by computer into distance jumped.

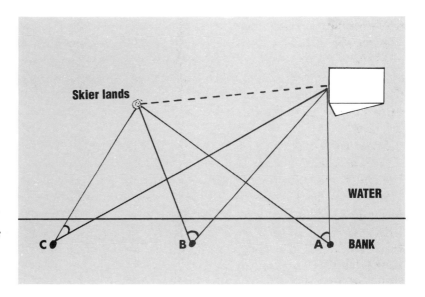

9. Look, no skis!

THE ultimate challenge for many skiers is to waterski without using skis. This is called barefooting.

The easiest way to learn this is by stepping off a slalom ski. (Your other option is to use a front step-off ski.) It is probably best to practise on a boom first, if one is available, because you can go that much slower and your falls will be less painful.

With the boat going at about 25 mph (40 km/h), hold onto the boom and ride on a slalom ski. Make sure the binding is very loose. Gently lower your back foot until you can feel the force of the water against the sole of your foot. Get the edge of the water in the arch of your foot and keep it there throughout the rest of the manœuvre. Slowly bend your ski leg and push your other leg forward, way out in front of the boom. When you get down into this 'plant' position, bending very low with one foot extended way out in front of you, and you can clearly feel the force of the water in the arch of your foot, then you simply cannot fall. The water has to rise above your toes to make you fall.

Gradually shift your weight over your extended leg. If you feel the edge of the water rising towards your toes, sit lower and extend

your foot further forward. Lean your whole body until your ski foot feels it is about to part company with its ski. As the ski comes off concentrate on keeping the water in the arch of your extended foot. Do not rush to put your other foot in the water; put it in cautiously, making sure the water goes into the arch of this second foot as well.

Once you can do this every time on the boom put the short rope on the boom. The only difference is you will have to concentrate much harder on balance. To calculate your speed as

Two-time world barefoot champion, Mike Seipel, steps off a ski and barefoots away. Perform this trick slowly and make sure the water is hitting the arch of your bare feet.

you go into the low plant position where you are sitting very low with your foot extended in front of you, take your weight in pounds, divide by 10 and add 20. Once the boat accelerates to this speed and you are sure you are low enough to keep the water in the arch of your foot, slowly follow through as you have learned directly on the boom.

On the long rope start at 30 mph (48 km/h) when you first put your foot in the water. Position yourself outside the wake so you are in the curl of the wake with your foot in the water banking up against the wake. The water is smoothest in this area. As you go into the low plant position the boat should accelerate up to the speed you have worked out with the formula and you should follow the exact steps learned on the boom. Remember, balance and getting down to the water are really important behind the boat. Keep down low and concentrate on your balance. This will allow the ski to come off more easily.

Then just get used to the feeling of skiing without skis.

10. Basic boat handling

YOU do not have to have a licence to drive or purchase a boat yet it can be as lethal and as dangerous as a car. There is nothing difficult in driving a boat but to do so safely and properly does require some forethought and training, particularly if you are towing a skier.

It is amazing the number of people who buy a sportsboat and then think where they are going to use it, only to find that (if they live inland) there are few stretches of water where powered craft are allowed and where there is no speed limit. So expect to trail your boat to the coast.

If you are unfamiliar with the area, try and reconnoitre the slipways that are available and find out the tidal (if appropriate) and weather conditions before you launch and also bear in mind what these will be when you want to recover your boat. The local coastguard station will have all this information on display as will most harbourmasters. Always tell someone where you are going and what time you expect to get there or return.

If you are at the coast or in a tidal estuary there are certain common sense items you should always carry with you. Lifejackets for all those aboard are obvious, but do make sure that they will fit your passengers. Children should wear lifejackets at all times and should be accompanied by an adult to supervise them. Ensure there is warm clothing aboard in case of an emergency. An anchor should always be carried as this will stop you drifting if you break down. A small, waterproof pack of flares could also be a lifesaver. If you plan to do a lot of coastal trips throughout the year then a radio is another safety item. Some spare rope, a sharp knife and a basic tool kit for your engine will all be used at some point even if not in an emergency.

Preparation for your boat and engine is essential before each trip as a breakdown can be both annoying and dangerous. It is best to have your engine serviced before the start of every season and at the same time have a thorough inspection of the mounting bracket(s) and the hull. Look for any holes or cracks where the gel coat has been broken. Then each time before the craft is used give it a quick once over to ensure everything is in order, paying extra attention to items that wear like the throttle and steering cables (if they are abnormally still or loose they could need replacing). If you have the time it is a good tip to tape a spare throttle and steering

cable alongside the existing ones so that these can be changed quickly. Always ensure that the boat's battery is fully charged as all the important functions of engine starting and bilge pumping and blowing are fully dependent on a healthy battery.

Before you launch at your chosen slipway do try and find out about any shallows and danger spots as well as the speed limits and areas of water you are allowed to use. There is precious little accessible water without speed or water-skiing restrictions so do not be the one responsible for losing another stretch! Having checked the tides and slipway for both launching and recovery and got your sportsboat on the water, proceed to an unrestricted area where you can enjoy the performance and handling of your craft.

There is nothing difficult about driving a boat but to do it safely you need to follow a few basic rules. Children should wear lifejackets at all times.

Boat handling and driving

Steering a sportsboat seems the same as steering a car, turn the wheel left and the boat goes left and vice versa. However there is a difference. To effect a steering manœuvre in a boat, instead of moving the front you are in fact pushing the back of the boat in the opposite direction to that in which you want the front to go. Since all sportsboats are steered by either moving the propulsion unit itself or by a moving rudder behind the propeller it will generally help the turn (there are exceptions)

if a bit more power is applied to increase the steering effect. This is the opposite to driving a car where you are generally braking to turn. Also remember that you are steering the back of the boat when leaving a dock: if you do not edge slowly away or give a good push off, the stern of the boat will hit the dock.

The first thing to do once you are clear of a dock is to check, at slow speed, which way your boat turns best in reverse. Because of the prop rotation, even with outboards and sterndrives, the boat will reverse better one way than the other and this will be important once you come to dock the boat. While mentioning reversing it is a good time to note that a good driver only ever uses reverse at tickover speed. Sportsboats are not designed to go backwards and hard reverse should only be used in an emergency.

Once under way, it is good driving to either keep the craft at tickover, where there is minimal wash, or properly on the plane. Don't drive at a speed where the boat is just off the plane as this produces the biggest wash which will annoy other water users. Unfortunately most speed limits seem to correspond to this latter situation and therefore defeat their purpose. When at speed remember that there are no set routes for you or other users to follow so craft will cross at many points. Keep alert and try to anticipate the actions of other water users. Since most sailing craft (including windsurfers) do not turn and go in the opposite direction that quickly it is best to go where they have been to play safe. Near land always keep a good lookout for swimmers as they are very hard to see. The best advice is: if you see any swimmers then do not go near that area.

Similarly, if there are any fishermen give them a wide berth as they may have cast their line a considerable distance and, besides annoying them, fishing line is hard to remove from your prop.

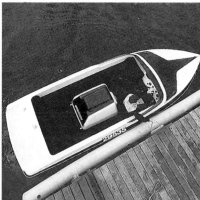

When coming in to land, never aim straight at the dock and always approach at a snail's pace.

If you show respect for other water users, who have just as much right to be on the water as you, then you will be a long way to being a good driver.

One of the keys to good boat driving is not being too flash. It is a big temptation to show off your boat by charging around at high speed but at the end of the day you will only impress other water users with your stupidity and lack of consideration.

If you want to drive fast and test your craft's handling find an unoccupied open stretch of water. Also remember that your passengers will probably not derive as much enjoyment from your fast driving and hard turns as you will. Boats can be very uncomfortable in rough conditions and passengers can take quite a pounding. If you need to convince the rest of the family as to the wisdom of your purchase this is not the best way to do it. Always ensure that your passengers are properly seated in the boat, not on it (on the edge) as a hard turn will easily throw them out. To prevent this you should not be carrying more passengers than there are seats.

At some point you are going to have to dock your boat and this can be one of the hardest manoeuvres you undertake. Remember that boats do not have brakes, they only have a reverse gear and, as I have already said, they are not designed to go backwards and should only be driven in reverse at slow speeds. You therefore have to allow plenty of distance for your boat to slow down and use the prevailing elements to help you slow the boat. For this reason you should always attempt to dock into a tide or wind and, if this is not possible, be aware of the speed of these two factors and allow extra distance. Never come straight at a dock as this will be the one time that your engine stalls and you ram the dock head on causing damage. Always come in at an angle so

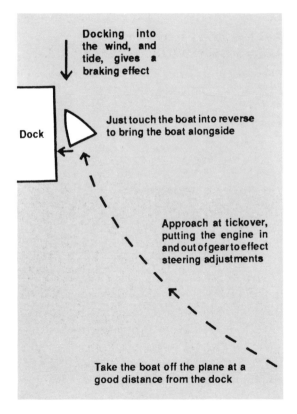

Docking into the wind, and tide, gives a braking effect

Just touch the boat into reverse to bring the boat alongside

Dock

Approach at tickover, putting the engine in and out of gear to effect steering adjustments

Take the boat off the plane at a good distance from the dock

steering but still keep the speed down. You will find that if the boat is not in gear there is a diminished steering effect. As you come to the dock at a snail's pace, just nudge the engine into reverse with the necessary lock to bring the boat parallel to the dock to moor. Try to dock so that this reversing procedure is in the direction where the boat naturally reverses (remember our reversing procedure earlier?).

Remember if there are waves, a tide or a cross wind from the side you will have to compensate for these in your angle of approach. There will be a temptation for any passengers, particularly children, to get up to hold the dock as you come alongside; do not let them until you say it is all right to do so. You may have to reverse hard if something goes wrong and this will throw them around in the boat; docking can also lead to trapped fingers if they do not know what they are doing. The driver is captain of his ship and all those aboard should do what he says to enjoy their boating.

Remember that the weather is everything to the safety and enjoyment of your sportsboating. Treat the conditions with respect and err on the side of caution in estimating the effects of the weather and the ability of your boat to cope with the conditions.

that, if something goes wrong, you will at least hit at a glancing angle. Slow the boat down a good distance away and come in at tickover putting the engine in and out of gear to effect

11. Towing a skier

TOWING a waterskier is like driving a 75-foot articulated lorry which is jack-knifing (the trailer is trying to go in front of the cab). With a boat you provide the pull for a skier who has a will and mind of his own but for whom you have to think. But the skier can only go where you want at the speed you want and so you have the responsibility for his safety and enjoyment.

There is no substitute for time in the driving seat but that must be allied to a feeling for

Boat drivers are responsible for a skier's safety and enjoyment.

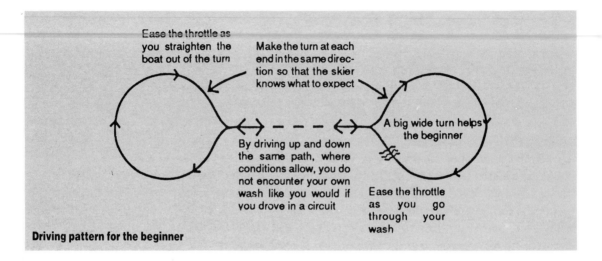

Ease the throttle as you straighten the boat out of the turn

Make the turn at each end in the same direction so that the skier knows what to expect

By driving up and down the same path, where conditions allow, you do not encounter your own wash like you would if you drove in a circuit

A big wide turn helps the beginner

Ease the throttle as you go through your wash

Driving pattern for the beginner

what the boat and skier are doing if you want to be a tournament boat driver working to hundredths of a second on the slalom and jump courses and to a quarter of a mile an hour for the trick skier.

Whatever standard of boat driving you aspire to, there are certain basic principles you must adhere to.

Perhaps the most demanding person to drive for is the beginner; good sympathetic driving can make his first lessons fun, hard uncaring driving can put him off for life. You will also get great enjoyment from helping a beginner to master the sport as his achievement is your achievement.

Driving for a beginner

Here I am only examining the role of the boat driver, not the instructor, although the two are often combined. Whatever standard of

skier you are towing you should always have someone in the boat with you to act as observer since you don't have eyes in the back of your head. The instructor will have prepared the skier with a dry land lesson to give him confidence and he is now in the water waiting to go.

If there is any wind or any waves, tow the beginner in the same direction as them, not against them. Not only will this make things easier for the skier but it is also easier to keep the boat straight when going with the wind and waves. You should also try to choose a course which gives the maximum length of flat unobstructed water before the boat has to turn. To ensure that you do not get rough water from your own wake drive to the pattern in the diagram. This maximises the length of flat water for the skier to use and learn on.

Before you start up the engine make sure

If the instructor holds the line before it has completely fed out, and pulls the skier at a slow speed, the skier will think he is starting. If the skier makes a mistake, the instructor can let go of the rope and the skier will sink down without losing the handle, so you can start again almost immediately.

that the skier is not too close behind as, besides the obvious danger of the propeller, you do not want to cover him with exhaust and engine fumes.

Pull away at tickover putting the boat in and out of gear as the line feeds out. Whilst at tickover it will save the beginner a fall or two if the instructor holds the line before it has completely fed out and pulls the skier at this slow speed. The skier thinks he is starting. If he makes a mistake the instructor lets go of the rope and the driver reverses gently. In this way the skier retains the handle and the instructor can correct the fault without the boat having to circle round the skier. Before the line goes tight, reverse a little so that the skier does not get pulled round. Then, once the instructor is satisfied with the pupil's position and you have checked everything is clear in front of you, apply smooth power to get the skier out of the water.

As the beginner comes onto the surface of the water (and the boat comes onto the plane) ease back the throttle so that the boat does not surge ahead and cause the skier to fall. The speed at which you tow the beginner will vary according to his size and the size of his skis. A good guide is to check that the skis are

tracking smoothly through the water, not ploughing or skittering on top.

If you have a good mirror fitted to the boat, use it because it is important always to be aware what the skier is doing while at the same time making sure your boat course is clear. If the skier wobbles slightly, an easing of the throttle will help him recover. Then gently reapply the power. Keep the boat's path straight so the skier stays in the middle of the wake. For the beginner, as for all standards of skier, the more power you have the easier it is to give a good tow, as long as you are sensible how you use it.

With your good driving and the instructor's tuition you will soon have the new skier in some form behind the boat.

The problem now is how to get the skier round the first corner. He does not know how to turn so you are going to have to drive him round. Make the turn as wide as possible and always keep the skier in the middle of the wake. This is done by increasing and decreasing the boat's speed. If the skier starts to go on the inside of the wake, a slight increase in boat speed will bring him back to the middle. If he starts to go on the outside of the wake (which is likely when you begin the turn and he keeps going straight), then a decrease in boat speed will drift him back to the middle of the wake. As you straighten the boat out of the turn, decrease the throttle slightly otherwise the speed will surge. Also ease the throttle when you go back through your own wash and keep the boat at this lower speed setting until the skier has cleared the wash. Easing the throttle will dip the vee shaped bow of the boat into the water and disperse the wake rather than slamming over it. This makes it easier for the skier and it gives a more comfortable ride to those in the boat.

Repeat this until it is time to take the skier back to the jetty. You have just helped teach someone to ski but you have not taught him how to stop (besides falling) and therefore you must take great care when returning him to dry land. The skier will always want to finish up just inches from the jetty so that he does not have to swim a stroke. As you turn in to the jetty, even if he has not learned to cross the wakes yet, he will try and pull for the jetty.

There are two things to remember here:

● Always tow a skier to finish alongside, not straight at, a jetty.
● You, as the driver, have full control over the skier. He has to be pulled by the boat otherwise he will sink. If you do not give him the pull then he will not be able to reach the jetty at a speed where he could hurt himself.

It is good advice therefore always to let a skier swim the last few yards to the jetty. The same applies if you are bringing him back to the beach: you should drop him off before the shallow water. Always ease back the power as the skier pulls towards the jetty. In that way he will not gain any speed to be able to coast to the jetty even if he lets go of the rope. You have full control over where he goes and at what speed; it is your fault if he hits the jetty. Once you have dropped your skier off always remember to drive to a safe area, stop and

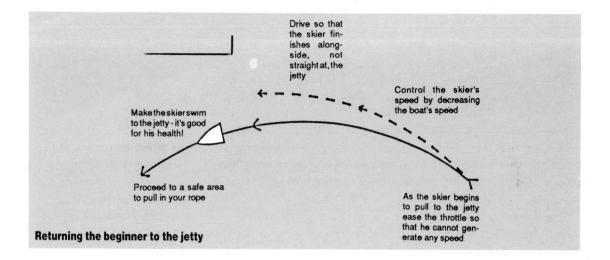

Drive so that the skier finishes alongside, not straight at, the jetty

Control the skier's speed by decreasing the boat's speed

Make the skier swim to the jetty - it's good for his health!

Proceed to a safe area to pull in your rope

As the skier begins to pull to the jetty ease the throttle so that he cannot generate any speed

Returning the beginner to the jetty

pull in your rope. Do not drive around with it left out.

Depending on his ability, either the first or second time on the water the beginner will be taught how to cross the wakes. A simple driving exercise can save falls and make this an easy exercise for the skier.

When a boat travels through the water it displaces water either side of it – this forms the wakes. When you go round a corner more water is pushed to the outside of the turn than the inside, creating a bigger wash on the outer wake. You can use this to make it easier for the skier to cross the wakes for the first few times. Driving on the main straight stretch of water you are using, put the boat on a gradual arced turn and increase the boat speed slightly to make it easier for the skier to pull to the inside of the gradual turn (where he would normally be losing speed). The skier then has a

much smaller wake to go over rather than having to climb up and fall down a high wake. As the skier gains in ability, straighten the boat so that he is going over a normal wake. Remember to make arced turns in both directions so that the skier gains experience at crossing both wakes.

Recovering a skier

Picking up a skier once he takes a fall is not as simple as you might think – especially when you have to take into account the wind and tide. Once the skier has fallen, bring your boat to a halt in a straight line and turn at tickover. You can then power back to your skier without sending any wash down your skiing lane for when you resume skiing. If there are other boats in the area, try to get back to your skier immediately as, separated from the boat, he will be hard to see.

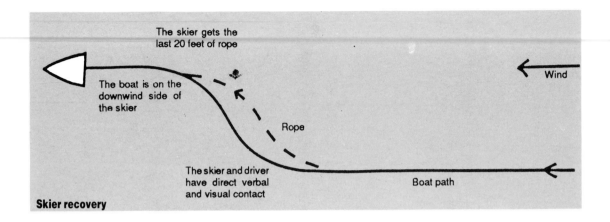

The skier gets the last 20 feet of rope

The boat is on the downwind side of the skier

Wind

Rope

The skier and driver have direct verbal and visual contact

Boat path

Skier recovery

Never head straight at the skier but aim to the side (just in case the steering goes) and take the boat off the plane a good distance before you reach him as he will not enjoy bobbing up and down in the water from your wash. If the conditions permit (to be explained in a moment), always approach the skier with him on your side so that you remain in visual and verbal contact at all times when you are near him. Try to be on the downwind side of him as a boat with high sides is going to be blown by the wind more than a skier with only his head sticking out of the water. If you were upwind of the skier and had to help him put his skis on you would get blown over him.

In practice, it is not always possible to come in downwind with the skier on your side so

Approach the skier on the driver's side so you are always in visual contact. Always approach slowly and allow for the wind and tide.

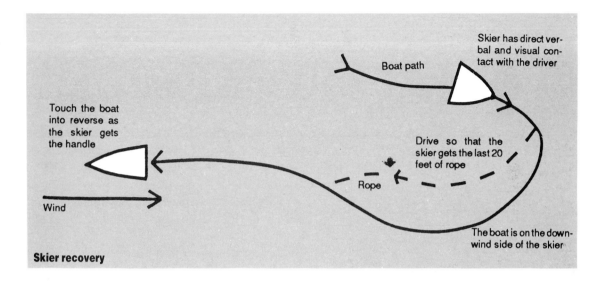

Skier has direct verbal and visual contact with the driver

Boat path

Touch the boat into reverse as the skier gets the handle

Drive so that the skier gets the last 20 feet of rope

Rope

Wind

The boat is on the downwind side of the skier

Skier recovery

you have to compromise. However, if you do come in upwind of the skier allow extra distance so you do not get blown over him.

Whichever way you want to proceed (with the wind if he is a beginner), try to drive so that the skier only gets the last 20 feet (6 m) of the rope; this prevents the water foaming as the inexperienced skier tries to pass the rope through his hands rather than letting it run through them. This is done by adjusting the tightness of the turn, if you are going to carry on skiing in the same direction, or by manoeuvring the boat if you are to ski in the opposite direction. Whichever direction, always put the boat into neutral and then give a touch of reverse as the handle comes to the skier. For a beginner this stops him being pulled sideways and wasting time and energy as he battles against the pull from the boat to

regain the skiing position. For the experienced skier this is a considerate touch which is the sign of a good driver.

Driving the intermediate skier

Once a skier can cross the wakes competently and has had a good grounding on two skis he should prepare to go mono by first lifting a ski. The instructor should run through the procedure on dry land. When driving for a skier lifting a ski set your boat speed slightly higher (approximately 1 mph (1.5 km/h) depending on the weight of the skier) as he is being supported by less ski area. When he is lifting the ski watch him carefully, easing the throttle if he gets into trouble so that he has more chance of recovering. When he is ready to drop the ski ensure that you have a long straight course and try to mark where he leaves the

When a skier has dropped a ski, the slightest jerk from the boat could cause a fall. Therefore, make any throttle adjustments minor and smooth.

drop ski, firstly so that you do not hit it on your return path and secondly to aid in its recovery.

The speed should be set the same as he had for lifting the ski and any throttle adjustments should be minor and very smooth as the slightest jerk from the boat will make the precariously balanced skier fall. Again, if he looks in trouble, ease the throttle slightly. The first corner should be driven as for the beginner: smoothly adjusting the boat speed

to keep the skier in the middle of the wake and easing the throttle when you go back through your own boat wakes to resume your course.

Falls are inevitable which means recovering the drop ski. Ensure that your skier is unhurt and that there are no boats in the vicinity before going to fetch the discarded ski from its marked position. Remember to take into account the wind and tide when looking for the ski.

When returning the mono skier to the jetty remember that he has little control and therefore control him as you come in and make him swim the last few yards.

The progression from there is the same as for the beginner with the arced turns to help him learn to cross the wakes and the increase in boat speed as he improves. The skier (and the driver) will soon get fed up with recovering the drop ski and, providing the skier is competent enough, the deepwater start should be taught.

The deepwater start

This is perhaps the hardest thing to drive and teach as it is difficult to see what the skier is doing. The driving technique is to bring the skier smoothly onto the surface of the water

Make the turns as big as possible for the novice mono skier, keeping him in the centre of the wakes by increasing and decreasing the boat's speed as necessary.

where he can keep control of the ski before pushing down and standing up.

If the skier has chosen to have two feet in the binding he will need more throttle than if he had only one foot in, because the ski is at a greater angle to the boat in the water. Once the skier is on the surface of the water and the boat is on the plane you will need to throttle back so that the ski tracks through the water properly and the pupil retains his balance. Again, smooth throttle control and a straight course are vital. Always be patient when the skier is preparing himself in the water because starting off when he is not ready is both tiring and frustrating for skier and boat driver alike.

The jetty start

Once the skier has mastered the deepwater start he will want to learn to start from the dock from a sitting or standing position so that he does not have to get into the water. Ensure that you drive straight away from the jetty in the direction that you want to go. If you make an arced turn away then the rope will do the same and, when you power away, the skier will not get a straight pull from the boat but an angled pull which will throw him off if he is inexperienced. Before you leave the jetty, place the rope in a visible position so that you can judge how much is left as you go out at tickover.

When you accelerate depends on the power of your boat, the weight of the skier, his size of ski and whether he is starting with one or two feet in the bindings, but always try to pluck your skier from the jetty, not pull him off. If you have a powerful boat then run out at tickover and accelerate as the rope pulls tight.

With a less powerful boat or heavier skier etc accelerate a bit earlier so that the boat is getting on the plane when the line goes tight. Remember to check in front of you before you power away that your course is clear. Keep the boat straight and, once the skier is on the water, ease back so that he can gain control of his ski. If he is struggling to stay up, a slight easing of the throttle will assist him.

A scooter start (where the skier is standing knee-deep in the water) is driven in the same way.

A jetty start puts pressure on both the driver and skier, especially when there is an audience, so always own up if you make a mistake and expect to get blamed if the skier falls despite your efforts to keep him up!

Conclusion

When asked whether skiers make the best drivers, the answer is usually yes as they are the ones who know how annoying bad driving can be. However, that does not mean that a non-skier cannot be a good driver as long as he is sympathetic to the skier's needs. That is the key to driving for all standards of skiing, smooth sympathetic throttle and boat control.

You have to think for the skier at all times, particularly when he is inexperienced. But, as a driver, you will have to accept that you will be the first to be blamed if the skier falls or has a bad ski and the last to be praised if the skier learns something new or skis well. Just remember, though, that it is a team effort and without you the skier is going nowhere.

12. Safety first

HERE are some safety reminders for drivers, observers and skiers. Follow them and your skiing trips will be safe as well as enjoyable.

- Skiers and children should always wear a buoyancy aid.
- The driver should always wait for the skier to shout 'Hit it' before starting. He should also make sure the ski tips are above water.
- Driver, skier and observer should know and understand the standard waterski hand signals which make communication between the skier and boat possible.
- The driver should make gradual turns over a wide arc.
- Always keep an alert lookout.
- When close to other ski boats, always turn to starboard.
- Be ready for an emergency. The driver and observer should sit in their seats – never on the deck or gunwhale.
- Remember, it is dangerous to ski in shallow water or too close to the shore.
- Do not ski in mooring areas or where there is a speed restriction.
- Do not ski at night, in the twilight or in bad weather.

Faster.

Slower.

Speed OK.

Cut engine (draw finger across throat).

Turn around (circular motion with finger).

Back to dock (pat head with flat palm).

● Do not ski near people fishing or swimming or other boats. Learn to recognise the warning buoys that indicate sub-aqua activity – and keep clear.
● Never try to cut ahead of any other boat, in case the skier falls in its path.
● Shut off the engine before helping the skier aboard.
● Come in to land slowly, preferably approaching on a near-parallel course.

I'm OK (after fall).

13. Equipment

ALL you need to go waterskiing is a boat with enough power to pull you, a tow-rope with a handle, a pair of skis or a mono ski, and a buoyancy aid. If it is cold you might also need a wetsuit or drysuit.

But don't rush out to buy these straight away. Borrow what you need until you know exactly what type of equipment you want.

Skis

Modern skis are made of hi-tech materials such as fibreglass, aluminium, carbon graphite and Kevlar. Some wooden skis are still made, mainly for beginners. Skis should fit snugly and be comfortable. The larger you are, the bigger your skis will need to be. The larger the skis, the easier it will be to get up.

There are four main types of skis: combination pairs, slalom, trick skis and jumpers. The first skis you try will probably be a pair of combos, with one ski set up with double binders. Later you can use this as a slalom ski.

The larger you are the bigger the skis you will need. Shown here are a pair of jump skis and a trick ski.

Different skis for different disciplines: trick ski, slalom ski and a pair of jump skis.

Slalom skis

Slalom skis can be categorised by price and performance. Generally, the most expensive skis are designed for the top skiers. Below these are skis aimed at recreational and novice mono skiers and intermediate level skiers.

Recreational-grade skis have a wider tail and flatter bottom, are easier to get up on and track easily when ridden straight.

As you progress and begin to make tighter turns and cut harder, you will need a ski with a more tapered tail, bevelled edges and a moderate concave or tunnel concave bottom.

Advanced skis are for tournament skiers who want help negotiating the course on a short line. These skis are designed to turn sharply and accelerate and decelerate quickly. But they are harder to get up on and do not ride well straight. These skis are usually fitted with high-wrap bindings which give the skier greater support and aid ski control. The fins of these skis are usually fitted with wings. These help the skier to decelerate quicker.

Trick skis

Trick skis are short and wide and feel very slippery to the beginner. They are finless so they are more difficult to control but they turn and slide more easily. Start on a less expensive pair and graduate to a top quality single trick ski.

Jump skis

Jump skis resemble the big, old-fashioned skis used in the early days of the sport. But, like slalom skis, they are made of the latest space-age materials. They have to be strong but light.

Towropes and handles

The standard rope length is 75 feet (22.86 m) and the standard handle is 12 inches (30.5 cm) wide. Slalom ropes have a number of take-off loops which make it easier to shorten the

One of the most essential pieces of equipment is a buoyancy aid. Make sure it is a good fit. Three- and four-buckle vests are best.

length when required. These are colour-coded to make it easier to recognise them at a glance.

Jump ropes are similiar to standard ropes but trick ropes are usually shorter – about 45 feet (13.7 m). Trick handles have toehold harnesses for toehold tricks. Another special piece of equipment for advanced trick skiers is a quick release. Mounted on the boat's ski pole, it can be released by the observer if the skier looks likely to become entangled in the rope after a fall.

Buoyancy aids

Today's ski vests are light, smart, comfortable and provide the necessary flotation. All skiers, apart from top trickers, should wear one. Three- and four-buckle vests are best.

Wetsuits and drysuits

Wetsuits let in a little water which warms up to your body temperature. Drysuits keep out the water but are bulkier. Both can be used to extend your skiing season. If it is very cold, you can also wear wetsuit gloves and hoods.

Wetsuits with built-in padding should always be worn to protect you while jumping or barefooting.

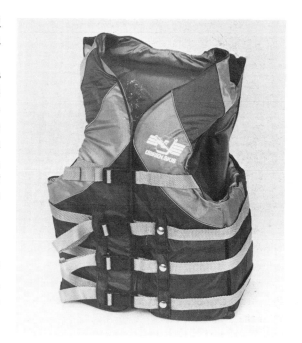

Ski gloves

Gloves are used to improve grip, especially useful when the skier is tired.

Helmets

Jumpers and ski racers should always wear an approved crash hat. Modern ones are very tough and very light.

Boats

Ski boats are 15–25 feet (4.5–6 m) in length with a suitable propeller and a 50–200 h.p. engine – powerful enough to pull up an adult on one ski from a deepwater start. To enable the driver to do his job well, a good ski boat should be easy to manœuvre at all speeds including tickover and offer good visibility. It should also have a ski mirror and easy-to-see, accurate speedos and information displays.

A sturdy ski pole and a rear-facing observer's seat are essentials for good ski boats.

The skier will appreciate a boat that creates crisp, even wakes at trick speeds, minimal wake at slalom and jump speeds and is easy to board from the water. Other highly desirable features include a rear-facing observer's seat, a sturdy ski pole and good storage space.

14. Further information

NOW that you know the basics, you should sign up for some lessons. For further information about waterskiing, lessons and clubs, contact one of the following:

- Jack Travers' International Tournament Skiing at Sun Set Lakes, PO Box 331, Okahumpka, FL 34762, USA. Tel: (904) 429 9027/(904) 324 3336.
- Waterski International, Brinkworth House, Brinkworth, Swindon, Wiltshire, England.
- British Water Ski Federation, 390 City Road, London EC1V 2QA. Tel: 01-833 2855.
- American Water Ski Association, 799 Overlook Drive, Winter Haven, FL 33884, USA.
- Australian Water Ski Association, PO Box 211, South Melbourne 3205, Australia.
- South African Water Ski Association, PO Box 90177, Bertsham, Johannesburg 2013, South Africa.
- Barefoot International, 2600 West Lantana Road, Lantana, Florida, USA.

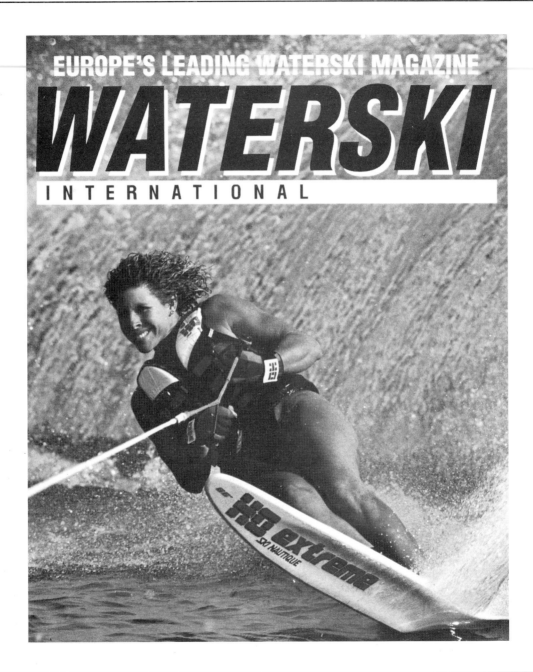